What is Trade?

Economics in Action

Carolyn Andrews

Crabtree Publishing Company
www.crabtreebooks.com

W9-CHX-451

Crabtree Publishing Company

www.crabtreebooks.com

Author: Carolyn Andrews
Coordinating editor: Chester Fisher
Series editor: Scholastic Ventures
Editor: Amanda Bishop
Proofreaders: Adrianna Morganelli, Crystal Sikkens
Project editor: Robert Walker
Production coordinator: Katherine Berti
Prepress technician: Katherine Berti
Project manager: Santosh Vasudevan (Q2AMEDIA)
Art direction: Dibakar Acharjee (Q2AMEDIA)
Cover design: Ranjan Singh (Q2AMEDIA)
Design: Ruchi Sharma (Q2AMEDIA)
Photo research: Anju Pathak (Q2AMEDIA)

Photographs:
123RF: Krzysztof Slusarczyk: p. 18 (bottom)
Alamy: Dennis Cox: p. 8; Euroluftbild de/Imagebroker: p. 29;
    David R. Frazier Photolibrary, Inc.: p. 5; The London Art
    Archive: p. 26; PeerPoint: p. 24
AP Images: Denis Poroy: p. 14; Marko Drobnjakovic: p. 15
BigStockPhoto: SCPhotog: p. 28; Verdandi: p. 11 (bottom left)
Dreamstime: Beisea: p. 21
Flicker: Carlojai: p. 27
Fotolia: Akalong: p. 18 (center); Nicolette Neish: p. 18 (top)
Getty Images: Nat Farbman/Time & Life Pictures: p. 19;
    Tom G. Lynn/Time & Life Pictures: p. 6; MPI/Stringer/
    Hulton Archive: p. 16
Istockphoto: p. 25; Biscut: p. 17 (bottom right); EnDen2005:
    p. 11 (bottom right); Floortje: p. 17 (center); Iofoto: p. 1, 7;
    Jaguar: p. 17 (top left); Peregrina: p. 17 (top right)
Jupiter Images: p. 4
Reuters: Finbarr O'Reilly: p. 12
Shutterstock: Agita: cover (left); Galyna Andrushko: p. 9;
    Arlene Jean Gee: p. 23; Patricia Hofmeester: p. 17 (bottom left);
    Pavel Losevsky: cover (center); Ljupco Smokovski: p. 22
TopFoto: Cresques Abraham/The British Library/HIP: p. 13

Illustrations:
Q2A Media Art Bank: p. 10, 20

Library and Archives Canada Cataloguing in Publication

Andrews, Carolyn, 1951-
    What is trade? / Carolyn Andrews.

(Economics in action)
Includes index.
ISBN 978-0-7787-4258-6 (bound).--ISBN 978-0-7787-4263-0 (pbk.)

    1. International trade--Juvenile literature. I. Title. II. Series:
Economics in action (St. Catherines, Ont.)

HF1379.A54 2008   j382   C2008-904154-2

Library of Congress Cataloging-in-Publication Data

Andrews, Carolyn.
  What is trade? / Carolyn Andrews.
    p. cm. -- (Economics in action)
  Includes index.
  ISBN-13: 978-0-7787-4263-0 (pbk. : alk. paper)
  ISBN-10: 0-7787-4263-6 (pbk. : alk. paper)
  ISBN-13: 978-0-7787-4258-6 (reinforced library binding : alk. paper)
  ISBN-10: 0-7787-4258-X (reinforced library binding : alk. paper)
  1. International trade. I. Title.

HF1379.A727 2009
382--dc22
                                    2008028979

Crabtree Publishing Company

www.crabtreebooks.com   1-800-387-7650

Printed in the U.S.A./102011/CG20110916

Published in Canada
Crabtree Publishing
616 Welland Ave.
St. Catharines, Ontario
L2M 5V6

Published in the United States
Crabtree Publishing
PMB 59051
350 Fifth Avenue, 59th Floor
New York, New York 10118

Published in the United Kingdom
Crabtree Publishing
Maritime House
Basin Road North, Hove
BN41 1WR

Published in Australia
Crabtree Publishing
3 Charles Street
Coburg North
VIC, 3058

Contents

Introduction   4

What is Trade?   6

Trade Leads to Exploration   8

Barter in the Americas   10

Gold-Salt Trade in West Africa   12

Barter Today   14

Trade with Money   16

Trade Between Nations   18

The U.S. as an Exporter Today   20

The U.S. as an Importer Today   22

Trade Between Other Nations   24

Tariffs   26

Tariffs Cause Conflicts   28

Glossary   30

Index and Webfinder   32

Introduction

Anna's shoes were too small. Her toes reached all the way to the tip. It was time to go shopping, so Mrs. Brown took Anna to the sporting goods store to buy her new shoes.

Choose What You Want

When they entered the store they saw many different items. Anna and Mrs. Brown headed toward the shoe department. When they arrived, they saw so many shoes, they were hard to count. Anna and her mother looked at each other and shrugged their shoulders.

"Now what do we do?" Anna asked.

A store clerk came to help them. Mrs. Brown told the clerk that Anna needed shoes.

"Well," said the clerk, "as you can see there are many choices. Do you have a particular style in mind? Are you looking for a special sport shoe or a shoe that can be worn for all occasions?"

Anna looked at her mom. She had no idea that there would be so many choices. Anna needed shoes she could wear to school, use in P.E., and play in after school.

▼ Stores offer many choices of products from all over the world.

The sales clerk took them to the shoe aisle. Anna looked up and down. The decision was difficult but finally Anna chose a pair. Anna tried the shoes on to make sure they fit. Mrs. Brown took them to the cashier and paid for the shoes.

"Mom, why are there so many choices?" Anna asked.

▲ Having so many choices makes shopping more interesting.

"One reason is because there are many different companies that make shoes. There are shoes made in many different countries, also. The United States buys shoes from all over the world. This gives everyone more choices," said Mrs. Brown.

"Clothing, food, oil, toys, and cars are just a few of the products that come into the U.S. every day from other countries. We are fortunate that we have so many choices. Not every country can say that," she continued. Mrs. Brown is correct. The U.S. buys and sells **goods** with many other countries. This way the country has many different products. These products make the country a better place to live. If it weren't for exchanging goods, the United States would not have so many choices.

FACT STOP

The first self-service grocery store was opened in 1916 in Memphis, TN. The owner thought it would save time if the customers picked out their own groceries. Now nearly all grocery stores are self-service, offering shoppers thousands of choices of foods.

What is Trade?

Mrs. Brown had a very good point. The United States sells products to other countries and buys products from many countries. The U.S. is involved in **trade**.

Trade, Goods, and Services

Trade is the exchange of goods and **services** for other goods and services or for money.

Goods are objects that people want or need. Services are actions or activities that one person does for another. If a group of people do not have access to certain goods or services, they search for other people to supply that good or service. Sometimes this involves traveling to far-away places. Other times the goods can be found from people who live nearby.

▼ These boys are trading sports cards.

▲ If it were not for trade, people in the U.S. would have very little coffee and chocolate.

Many boys and girls collect baseball cards. Sometimes to finish a collection, a young person will trade a card they have for a card they need. Both people in the trade get what they want, so they have better sets of cards than they did before the trade.

Trade gives people more choices. For example, fruits and vegetables grow only in the summer months in most of the U.S. So much of the fruit that people in the U.S. eat is grown in the countries of South America. Without trade, fruits like grapes, bananas, and oranges would not be available here in the winter months.

Trade also helps people get products they would not have at all. People in the United States like chocolate and coffee. Chocolate is made from cacao beans that grow in South America. Coffee is grown in the mountains of South America. By trading for these things, Americans get the chocolate and coffee they love.

FACT STOP

The first baseball cards were put in cigarette boxes. The most valuable card is the Honus Wagner card. He did not like smoking, so his card was removed from the boxes. Only a few of his cards were ever found.

Trade Leads to Exploration

Trade has helped people meet and share goods and ideas. If a people needed things they did not produce, they would travel in search of other people who had those products. This travel led to the exploration of places all around the world.

Early Trade

Some of the earliest traders were the Aramaeans (AR uh MEE uhnz) and the Phoenicians (fih NEE shuhnz). The Aramaeans used **caravans**, groups of people who travel together carrying goods, to cross the area of the Middle East known as the Fertile Crescent. They traded goods and shared their language, Aramaic (ar uh MEY ik).

The Phoenicians traveled by sea. They reached southern Spain and the western coast of Africa. They exchanged cedar logs, purple cloth, glass objects, and jewelry for precious metals like gold and silver. To keep better records of trade, they invented an alphabet using letters to represent sounds. This system is called the "Mother of the Modern Alphabet." Today, most countries of the world use an alphabet.

People in ancient China were not in contact with other cultures for many centuries. In 139 B.C.E., the emperor of China sent General Zhang Qian (JAHNG CHYEN) on an expedition. Upon his return in 126 B.C.E., he told stories of a people who had short hair, wore strange garments and rode in chariots.

▼ This statue represents Chinese traders on the **Silk Road**.

 Camels were the perfect animals for Aramaeans trading in the Fertile Crescent.

Zhang's travels led to the trade routes known as the Silk Road. The Silk Road went from the Pacific coast of China to the Mediterranean Sea. Chinese traders exchanged silk for gold, glassware, wool, and linen with traders from the Middle East.

Christopher Columbus explored to find an easier trade route to the countries of the Far East. He thought that if he sailed west, he could reach India faster. Instead, he discovered North and South America. Other explorers traveled to the Americas to search for precious metals. They found gold and other products that Europe did not have. Imagine tasting chocolate, tomatoes, or potatoes for the first time! These products quickly came into demand in Europe. As a result, people from Europe came to the Americas to live. Many became involved in trade.

FACT STOP

Zhang Qian's journey to the west and back took 13 years. Many of his soldiers were killed by **barbarians**. Barbarians were people who did not have an advanced way of life. Zhang spent ten years as a prisoner of these barbarians.

Barter in the Americas

Many early people did not have coins or money with which to buy things. Instead, they offered something that they had for something that they needed or wanted. This type of trade is called **barter**.

The Maya and Inca

The Maya were a group of people who lived in Mexico and Central America. They grew many different crops including maize, tomatoes, chili peppers, beans, and squash. Their skilled farming methods helped them to grow many crops.

Farmers brought their extra crops to the open markets in cities. There they would exchange them for cotton cloth, pottery, fish, salt, and objects made of **jade**.

Mayan **merchants**, people who exchange goods as a job, traveled throughout Mexico and Central America trading goods. They traded maize, pumpkins, chili peppers, tomatoes, feathers, cocoa, and honey for cotton cloth, objects made of jade, pottery, fish, deer meat, and salt. The merchants traveled mainly by canoes. If the merchants traveled on land, they needed people to carry the goods. The Mayans never developed wheels or learned to use animals to carry loads.

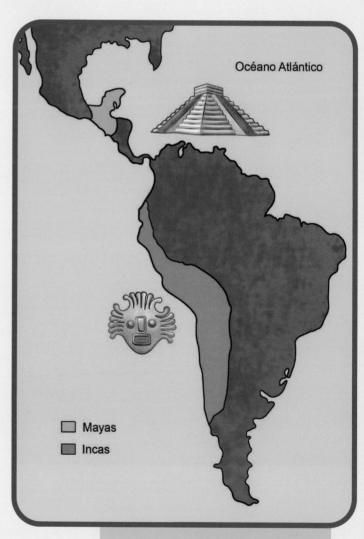

Océano Atlántico

☐ Mayas
☐ Incas

▲ The Maya and Inca nations were located where Mexico and Central America are found today.

10

The Inca lived in South America in what is now Peru and Chile. They were ruled by an emperor who controlled the lives of the people. The emperor told farmers which crops to plant and how much to plant. Their main crops were potatoes and a grain call **quinoa** (kee NOH uh). After each harvest, food was collected in central places and then given out to the people. The food was shared so that everyone had enough to eat. Any extra could be used in trade. The roads built throughout the empire made it easier to collect, hand out, and trade the food.

There were many Inca merchants. Some traded copper for red seashells. Others traded salted dried fish, clothes, beads, cotton, beans, and other things. Inca merchants traded everything by barter. No coins or money were ever involved.

FACT STOP

The Inca built 12,000 miles of roads though the forests and mountains to link their empire together. Relay runners traveled the roads carrying news from one place to another. This system of roads helped to make the empire strong.

▶ Maize (right) is related to the corn we eat today.

Gold-Salt
Trade in West Africa

Between 300 C.E. and 1600 C.E., three great trading kingdoms rose and fell in West Africa. Each kingdom built its wealth by trading gold for salt. Salt was needed to preserve and flavor food. People traveled great distances to get it.

Kingdoms Build on Salt

The first kingdom, Ghana (GAH nuh), was located between the salt mines of the Sahara Desert and the gold mines of the forests of Africa. Caravans from North Africa brought salt, swords, and cloth to Ghana. Ghanaian (GAH nee uhn) merchants took kola nuts and farm products north to Morocco (muh ROK oh). **Muslim** (MUHZ lim) traders brought salt and traded for Ghanaian gold. Muslims are people who follow the teachings of **Mohammad** and believe in only one God, Allah.

The salt and gold trade brought new ideas into Ghana. Many Ghanaians accepted Muslim customs.

Soon attacks by outsiders led to the end of the kingdom. Many groups of Ghanaians formed small kingdoms. One kingdom, Mali (MAH lee), began to conquer nearby kingdoms. By the late 1200s, Mali was becoming powerful; they began the gold-salt trade again.

▼ Salt mines are still used all over the world to produce salt.

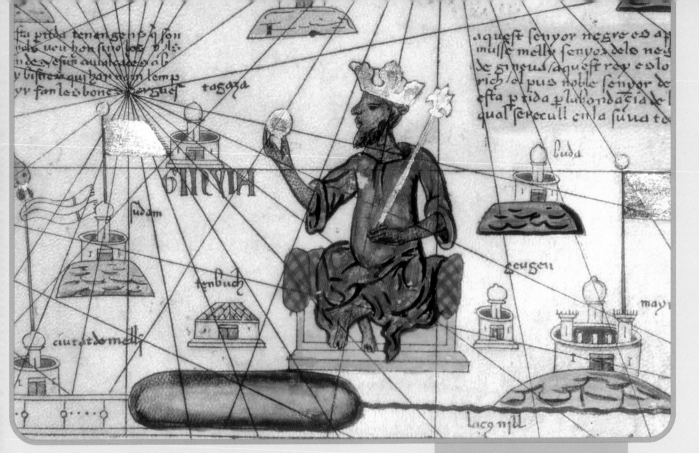

The following text appears within the illustration: tagaza · GINEVA · fudam · tenbuch · ciutat de melly · buda · geugeu · mayr · lacg nill · and handwritten text in the upper corners: "stu p... tenen gen... son nole ueu hon fino uot... y... in de o efur anla...aco af... y bifter equi han... tem... yr fan leebone... guef" (left) and "aquest fenyor negre es... muffe melly fenyor delo neg de ginena/aquest rey e... rich/el pus noble fenyor de efta p...rida p la bondacia le qual fe reculi en la fuua to..." (right)

▲ King Mansa Musa build the kingdom of Mali by trading salt and gold.

The greatest king of Mali was **Mansa Musa** (1312-1337). He opened trade routes and sent soldiers with caravans to protect the traders and goods. Mali continued to get richer. After a trip to **Makkah** (MAK kuh), a city in Arabia, Mansa Musa brought architects and teachers to Mali. Great buildings were built and learning increased.

After Mansa Musa died, Mali came under attack. The kingdom soon divided into independent kingdoms. One of these kingdoms was Songhai (song GAHY).

Songhai became a great, wealthy kingdom because of the gold trade. Soon, neighboring kingdoms became jealous of Songhai's wealth. In 1590, the leader of Morocco sent his armies to Songhai. The Songhai soldiers fought with swords, spears, and bow and arrows. The Moroccans (muh ROK uhns) had guns and cannons. Songhai was defeated and the empire ended.

FACT STOP

There are salt mines all over the world. One of the oldest salt mines still in use is in Poland. People have been mining salt there for over 900 years. Visitors go underground and visit the museum, chapels, and lakes located there. Sometimes, concerts are held in the large chambers.

Barter Today

Barter is still used in some places today. Many people would rather trade something they have than to pay money. These people like to attend **"swap meets."** A swap meet is a place where people gather to exchange goods.

At the Swap Meet

Swap meets are held outside or in large buildings. People set up booths and display the things they want to exchange. Some swap meets concentrate on just a few types of items. Others are open for anything that someone might want to trade.

People who like antique and classic cars can visit swap meets in Springfield, Ohio, Portland, Oregon, New Braunfels, Texas, or Reno, Nevada. If you need a motorcycle or parts, go to the swap meets held around Michigan.

One of the largest swap meets is held in Aloha Stadium in Hawaii. It boasts that it has "over 700 vendors, crafters, and artists from all over the world."

▼ Goods of all kinds are exchanged at swap meets.

▲ When people trade or barter, each person gets something they want.

Students also take part in trading by barter. How many times have you traded the apple in your lunch for a cookie or cupcake? Students trade pens for pencils or paper.

People also trade toys and games. Old toys, lunch boxes, and dolls are just a few of the things people collect and trade with other people. A lot of this trading goes on over the Internet. There are special websites just for trading.

Some people also barter services. Some parents trade babysitting with other parents for time for work and errands. Teenagers may clean the house in order to use the family car. Children trade chores in order to get to do the chore they like best.

FACT STOP

A swap meet has been held in New Braunfels, Texas, every year since 1992. People from many different places come together to swap parts for old cars.

Trade With Money

Even though many people bartered, this was not always the best way to trade. Sometimes, a person who wanted to trade did not have the item that another person wanted. A better way to trade developed. This form of trade used coins or paper money. With coins, a person could buy what he wanted instead of exchanging an item for it.

Coins, Paper, and More

The first coins were used by the Lydians (lid E uhnz). They lived in a region of Iraq, located between the Tigris and Euphrates rivers, called Ancient Mesopotamia (mes uh puh TEY mee uh). The coins were made from a mixture of gold and silver. They were stamped with a drawing of a lion's head.

The use of coins spread to Greece and other parts of the world. Many cities made their own coins and put pictures on them to show pride in the city. The Romans put the picture of their ruler on the coins they made.

If precious metals like gold or silver were not available to make into coins, people would use other objects. The objects were usually difficult to get or there were not many available. This made the coins valuable.

▼ **Wampum** was strung together in fanciful patterns.

▲ Most countries produce their own currency. Some countries in Europe share a currency, called the Euro.

Native Americans on the Atlantic coast used shells to show their wealth. These shells were difficult to get. It took many hours to polish the shells before they were placed on strings or woven into belts. The strings and belts of shells were called wampum. It was not until settlers from England came to America that wampum was used as money. Wampum was used to buy tools, animal skins, furs, canoes, and other items. The use of wampum spread to Ohio, Illinois, and the Great Plains.

Today, most people use coins or paper money to buy and sell goods. This money is called **currency**. Each country prints paper money and makes coins. Currency in the United States is the dollar; in Japan, the yen; and in Europe, the Euro. The money is given a value, and people use the money to buy the things they want and need.

FACT STOP

Wampum was in two colors, white and purple. The white shells came from a large sea snail called the whelk. The purple shells came from a saltwater clam called the quahog. The purple shells were worth two times as much as the white shells.

Trade Between Nations

People began to come to the **New World** to live. European countries set up **colonies**, settlements formed and ruled by a country in another land. **Plantations**, or large farms, grew crops like sugar, coffee, and cotton that were needed in Europe. As more workers were needed, **colonists**, people who settled in the colonies, turned to Africa as a source of workers.

Triangular Trade

Traders began to bring Africans to the New World to work as **slaves**. Slaves are people who are owned and controlled by other people. Slaves have no rights or freedoms. They do what they are told or they are severely punished.

Trade between Africa, Europe, and the Americas was called **triangular trade**. Traders took rum, molasses, tobacco, and other products to Europe. These were sold, and traders used the money to buy guns, ammunitions, and cloth. These products were taken to Africa and exchanged for human laborers. Hundreds of Africans were crammed on ships and taken across the Atlantic Ocean. The voyage became known as the **Middle Passage**. Once in the Americas, the Africans were sold into slavery. Triangular trade continued until the late 1800s.

▲ Early traders did business with fur, grain, and tobacco.

▲ During World War II, the U.S. traded jeeps to countries that needed vehicles in battle.

As the colonies grew, so did the trade. The colonies on the Atlantic Coast of North America, exchanged many goods with England. England wanted the colonies to trade only with them. This caused problems, and was part of the cause of the American Revolution.

Settlers also traded with Native Americans. They traded iron pots and steel knives for furs. Trade led to disagreements between the French and English, and even caused a war.

After the United States became a nation, trade with other nations continued. The United States became involved in two world wars during the twentieth century. During both wars, the U.S. shipped food and war supplies to countries in Europe. The people in the U.S. chose to do without some things and use less of others. Gas, sugar, wheat, coffee, meat, butter, and shoes were not always available. Instead, they were needed for the people fighting the wars in Europe.

FACT STOP
England taxed items such as sugar, molasses, and tea that were shipped into the colonies. This is one of the reasons the American colonists rebelled against England.

The U.S. as an Exporter Today

Ships, trains, and trucks leave the United States every day loaded with tons of goods. These goods are shipped to countries all over the world. The United States is one of the leading **exporters** in the world. An **export** is a good sold to another country. An exporter is a person or country that sells goods to other countries.

▼ These states export more goods than any other.

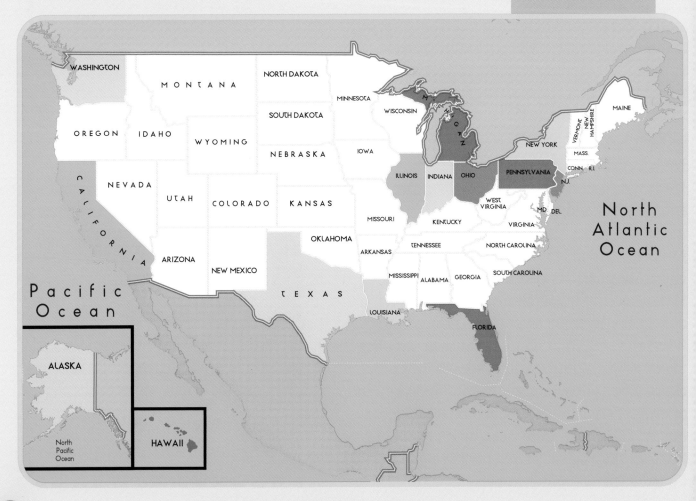

We Make What Others Need

The United States has hundreds of factories that make many different goods. There are many farms in the U.S. that produce too many crops for the people to use. Since the people do not use all the goods that are made and grown, companies sell these products to other countries that need them.

Many countries that buy goods from the U.S. are not able to grow enough food for their people. Some do not have the **natural resources** to make the goods they need. Other countries buy goods from the U.S. because the U.S. buys goods from them. Trade helps keep countries friendly with each other.

▲ Ships take grains from the U.S. to countries such as Japan who are unable to grow all that they need.

Each state in the U.S. sells goods to other countries. The states that sell the most are Texas, California, New York, Washington, Illinois, Florida, Michigan, Ohio, New Jersey, Louisiana, Pennsylvania, and Indiana.

These states, along with all the others, sell many different items. These goods include meat, dairy products, soybeans, cotton, machinery, and chemicals. The U.S. also produces **telecommunications equipment**, radio, television, satellite equipment used for sending information around the world.

Many companies send people around the world to teach countries how to use the machines that they buy. In this way, the U.S. also exports services.

Education, health care, and banking services are exported. Teachers help other teachers learn new ways of teaching, and sometimes teach students how to speak English. American doctors show other doctors how to treat illnesses and use new medicines. Bankers and accountants help companies learn how to manage the money they make.

FACT STOP

In 2007, Texas exported more goods than any other state in the United States. The state that exported the fewest amount of goods was Hawaii.

The U.S. as an Importer Today

Not only does the United States export goods, it **imports** goods as well. A nation that imports brings in goods from other countries to sell. The United States imports more goods than any other country.

We Buy What We Need

The United States has many natural resources. U.S. farmers grow more food than most countries in the world. Factories in the U.S. make almost anything a person could want or need. So why does the United States import so many goods? The answer is complicated.

One reason is to get goods that cannot be grown or produced in the United States. An example of these would be coffee and chocolate. As you have read, these items grow in the countries of South America. Importing coffee and chocolate allows Americans to have what they want.

The United States imports some goods because it is often cheaper to make the goods in other countries. Workers in China and Mexico get paid less money than in the U.S. When we buy goods from these countries, we can pay less for the product.

▼ More electronics are made in Japan, so they are shipped to the U.S. for sale.

Importing goods from other countries helps those countries' economies. When the U.S. buys goods from Vietnam or India, it is helping by giving people there jobs. They can then buy goods for their families so they can live better.

The United States wants to be friendly with other countries. When countries trade with each other, they get along better. Countries that trade with each other are less likely to go to war. In fact, countries punish other countries by stopping trade.

Oil is one item the United States imports. It imports oil from many countries including Canada, Mexico, Saudi Arabia, and other countries of the Middle East.

Mexico also sells fruit, vegetables, tin, gold, sugar, car parts, and clocks to the United States. China sells toys, clothing, and shoes to the U.S. From India, the U.S. buys jewelry and clothing. Japan sells televisions and other electronic items, cars, and motorcycles to the United States. The U.S. buys goods from many countries in Africa, Europe, Asia, and South America.

▼ Oil ships from Canada to the U.S., where it is made into gasoline or other petroleum products.

Trade Between Other Nations

Many countries **specialize** in things that they exchange with other countries. If a country specializes, it produces large amounts of a few items. They then buy the other things that they need from their **trading partners**, or countries they trade with. Chinese factories produce many different items, but they mainly trade toys and clothing. Saudi Arabia exports mainly petroleum. These items are traded all over the world.

How Nations Choose Trading Partners

The United States does not trade with Cuba, an island nation near Florida, because they do not give people much freedom. Cuba sells its famous cigars, sugar, and nickel to many other countries. Cuba's biggest trading partners are Venezuela and China. Cuba buys the goods it needs from countries other than the United States.

▼ These workers in China use **raw materials** to make toys.

▲ Japan must get its oil shipped from other countries.

In September, 1960, Iran, Iraq, Kuwait, Saudi Arabia, and Venezuela, formed the **Organization of Petroleum Exporting Countries**, or **OPEC**. OPEC was formed to make sure there was enough oil for countries to use and to help keep prices from changing too much. This organization now has 13 members. Together they export oil to almost every country in the world. These countries specialize in trading petroleum.

Japan has few natural resources and very little farm land. Because of this, Japan imports food, oil, chemicals, cloth and raw materials from China, the United States, Saudi Arabia, Australia, and South Korea. Examples of raw materials would be cotton, steel, and plastic, which can be used to make clothing, cars, and toys. Japan uses the raw materials to make goods that can be exported. Japan exports cars, chemicals, and electronics to countries like China, South Korea, and the United States.

FACT STOP

Japan has almost no oil resources. It imports most of its oil from the countries of the Persian Gulf.

Tariffs

A **tariff** is a tax placed on goods that are imported into a country. Tariffs protect the producers of goods within the country. A tariff makes the imported good cost more so people will not buy as much of it. Instead, they will buy the cheaper good that is produced within the country.

The History of Tariffs

Tariffs have been in use for many years. The English colonies of North America were forced to pay tariffs on items such as tea, molasses, and sugar. The tax on tea led to the Boston Tea Party. Colonists who were against the tariff went aboard a ship in the Boston Harbor and dumped boxes of tea into the water.

▼ The Boston Tea Party was a protest against British tariffs on tea.

Tariffs are also a way of raising money for the government of a country. The money is collected and put into the treasury. It is then used to improve trade, build roads, or help people.

Tariffs are a percentage of the cost of the good. For example, a manufacturer from Cambodia sells a pair of sneakers for $12.00 to an American importer. The tariff is 20%, or $2.40. The importer must pay $14.40 for the sneakers.

Sometimes, countries make agreements with each other to end tariffs on certain goods. These agreements are called **trade agreements**. The United States has trade agreements with 14 different countries. Each agreement lets the countries trade with each other. They pay lower tariffs or none at all.

In 1992, the United States, Mexico, and Canada began an agreement that would eventually end all tariffs on goods shipped between the three countries. The agreement went into effect on January 1, 1994. The items would have to be made of materials produced only in U.S., Mexico, and Canada. Gradually, over 15 years, the tariffs on these goods would be reduced and finally ended. The agreement is the **North American Free Trade Agreement**, or **NAFTA**. The purpose of NAFTA is to increase trade between the three countries.

FACT STOP

The Affordable Footwear Act was introduced to Congress in December, 2007. The purpose of this bill is to end the tariff on children's shoes. Many companies are for the bill because it would lower prices.

▼ Tariffs were removed from children's shoes so they are more affordable to families.

Tariffs Cause Conflicts

Even though tariffs are supposed to help a country, sometimes they cause tariff disputes. These disputes are called **trade wars**.

Trade Wars Start

In 1930, the United States increased its tariffs on all products coming into the country. The countries that traded with the U.S. also raised their tariffs. Trade between the U.S. and other countries decreased. This hurt the U.S. and the countries the U.S. traded with.

▼ Tariffs on banana imports to Europe started the **Banana Wars**.

Frozen chickens were the next item that caused a dispute. European countries raised the tariff on chickens imported from the U.S. The U.S. then raised tariffs on goods from France, Holland, and Germany.

In 1985, the U.S. put tariffs on pasta from Europe. Europe got back at the U.S. by increasing tariffs on lemons and walnuts.

Bananas became the center of a trade war. American fruit companies grow bananas on farms in Latin America. The U.S. sells these bananas to countries around the world. In 1993, the **European Union**, or **EU**, raised the tariffs on bananas that were exported by American and Latin American fruit companies. The European Union is a group of countries who trade as one country. When the fruit companies complained to the U.S. government about the high tariffs, it raised the tariffs on goods imported by the U.S. from the EU. These items included dolls, coffee makers, plastic purses, and bath oils. This was the beginning of the Banana Wars.

The disagreement grew. Certain beef imported from the U.S. was banned in Europe. So the U.S. put tariffs on European clothing and some cheeses, meats, and mustards.

Both sides of the dispute took their problems to the **World Trade Organization (WTO)**. The World Trade Organization was founded in 1995 to help nations form trade agreements and solve disputes. After many meetings, an agreement was reached. The European Union agreed to allow fruit companies to export bananas to the EU. The U.S. lowered the tariffs on European goods.

▲ The World Trade Organization has its headquarters in Geneva, Switzerland.

FACT STOP

According to the World Trade Organization, it takes about 15 months to settle a trade dispute. There have been about 300 disputes brought before the WTO since 1995 by the 151 member nations.

Glossary

American Revolution The battle between Great Britain and the American colonies in 1775-1783

Banana Wars Trade dispute between the United States and the European Union

barbarians People who did not have an advanced way of life

barter A type of trade where a good or service is exchanged for another good or service

caravans Groups of people who travel together carrying goods

colonies Settlements formed and ruled by a country in another land

colonists People who settled in the colonies

currency Coins or paper money

European Union (EU) Group of countries in Europe who trade as one country

export A good sold to another country

exporter A person or country that sells goods to other countries

goods Objects that people want or need

imports Goods brought into a country from other countries to sell

jade A valuable green stone

Makkah A city in Arabia considered holy by the Muslims

Mansa Musa The greatest king of Mali. He expanded trade and made a trip to Makkah

merchants People who exchange goods as a job

New World North and South America

Middle Passage Voyage of slaves across the Atlantic Ocean from Africa

Mohammad The founder of Islam

Muslim People who follow the teachings of Mohammad and believe in only one God, Allah

NAFTA (North American Free Trade Agreement) An agreement between the United States, Canada, and Mexico to end tariffs on goods shipped between the countries

natural resources Things that occur on or in the earth from which other goods can be made; examples: trees, iron, gold, tin, coal

OPEC (Organization of Petroleum Exporting Countries) A group of 13 countries that work together to produce and export oil around the world

plantations Large farms that grow crops like sugar, coffee, tobacco, and cotton

quinoa A grain-like plant grown in South America

raw materials Items that can be used to make other things

services Actions or activities that one person does for another

Silk Road A trade route that went from the Pacific coast of China to the Mediterranean Sea

slaves People who are owned and controlled by other people

specialize To devote one's efforts into one or a few activities or area of work

swap meet Place where people gather to exchange goods

tariff A tax or duty placed on goods that are imported into a country

telecommunications equipment Radio, television, and satellite equipment used for sending information around the world

trade The exchange of goods and services for other goods and services or for money

trade agreements Agreements between countries to end or lower tariffs on imports

trade war A disagreement between countries over tariffs or taxes on imported goods

trading partners Countries that trade with each other

triangular trade Trade between Africa, Europe, and the Americas

wampum The strings and belts made of shells used as money by Native Americans

World Trade Organization (WTO) An organization that helps nations form trade agreements and solve disputes

Index

Ancient Mesopotamia 16
Aramaeans 8, 9

Banana Wars 28, 29
barbarians 9
barter 10, 11, 14, 15, 16

cacao beans 7
caravan 8, 12, 13
chocolate 7, 9, 22
coffee 7, 18, 19, 22, 29
colonies 18, 19, 26
colonists 18, 19, 26
Columbus, Christopher 9
currency 17

European Union (EU) 29
exports 20, 21, 22, 24,
    25, 29

gold 8, 9, 12, 13, 16, 23
Gold-Salt Trade 12, 13

imports 22, 23, 25, 26,
    27, 28, 29
Inca 10, 11

jade 10

Lydians 16

Makkah 13
Mali 12, 13
Mansa Musa 13
Maya 10
merchants 10, 11, 12
Middle Passage 18
Mohammad 12
money 6, 10, 11, 14,
    16-17, 18, 21, 22, 27
Morocco 12, 13
Muslim 12

Native Americans 17, 19
natural resources 21,
    22, 25
North American Free Trade
    Agreement (NAFTA) 27

oil 5, 23, 25
Organization of Petroleum
    Exporting Countries
    (OPEC) 25

Phoenicians 8
plantations 18

quinoa 11

raw materials
    24, 25

services 6, 15, 21
Silk Road 8, 9
slaves 18
Songhai 13
swap meet 14, 15

tariff 26, 27, 28, 29
trade agreement
    27, 29
trade war 28, 29
trading partner 24
triangular trade 18

wampum 16, 17
World Trade Organization
    (WTO) 29

Zhang Qian 8, 9

Webfinder

https://www.cia.gov/library/publications/the-world-factbook/index.html
http://www.wto.org/index.htm
http://www.opec.org/home/
http://www.fas.usda.gov/info/factsheets/NAFTA.asp
http://nabataea.net/fun1.html